GOD'S HARVEST

God's Harvest

The nature of true revival

I. D. E. Thomas

Gwasg **Bryntirion** Press
(formerly Evangelical Press of Wales)

Unless otherwise stated, Scripture quotations in this publication
are from the Holy Bible, Authorized Version

Cover photo: Eric Dresser
Cover design: burgum boorman ltd.

Published by
Gwasg **Bryntirion** Press
(formerly Evangelical Press of Wales)
Bryntirion, Bridgend CF31 4DX, Wales, UK
Printed by Creative Print and Design (Wales), Ebbw Vale

Contents

Foreword
to the first edition

I count it a privilege to commend this booklet. It was born, I think, from the Jubilee of the Welsh Revival of 1904–05. I know there are some who are disposed to dismiss that Awakening as ephemeral and effervescent. There are two reasons why I have been obliged to take a more serious view of it. First, I was cradled near its birthplace and I have met and learned to revere those who were plucked as brands from the burning during the revival. Even as a boy I recognized in them the fragrance and unction of men who knew God in a way which made them quite different from the ordinary run of Christians.

Secondly, I am now closely associated with the work of Charlotte Chapel in Edinburgh. It is no secret that Charlotte Chapel has been a crowded church for more than half-a-century—the numbers have scarcely fluctuated during all this time, but what is not so widely known is that Charlotte Chapel came very near to being abandoned at the turn of the century as a finished cause. It was an experience of revival which rescued the church from the fate of being sold as a city warehouse for one of the Princes Street shops, and transformed it into a centre of exultant evangelism. I think it is relevant to the purpose of this book that I should humbly place this on record, to the sole glory of God and for our encouragement today. This

Edinburgh revival will be for ever linked with the name of Joseph Kemp, the then pastor, but, as his biography shows, the fires of revival were kindled in his heart through his contact with the Welsh Revival and Evan Roberts. The similarity between the Welsh Revival and the Kemp Revival is very marked indeed, and it is true to say that this church is one of the lasting monuments to the reality of the 1904 Awakening. Of course there is not one of us who could not have wished that that revival had gone deeper and further!

The subject of revival is again a vital issue. One of the historians of our day has given it as his judgment that only a world-wide spiritual renewal can save our generation from disaster. This book treats the question of revival with knowledge and scriptural insight. It attempts no blueprint, nor does it send up a sentimental cry for John Wesley or Jonathan Edwards, or any other bygone revivalist, raised from the dead. It recognizes that God fulfils himself in many ways, and does not attempt to limit the methods of divine awakening. But it stresses with clarity and eloquence the *permanent* elements in every spiritual renewal.

It recalls us to evangelism as the primary and paramount task of the Church. It is useless to expect the leaven of the gospel to transform society until it has done its converting work in men's hearts. It recalls us, too, to the first mark of the New Testament Church—'Holiness, without which no man shall see the Lord' (Gen. 12:14). No amount of Christian organization and effort can be a substitute for a Holy Church. As P. T. Forsyth once expressed it—'Holiness is the one thing damnatory to the power of Satan.' And our supreme need as Christian people today is the rediscovery and practice of scriptural holiness.

I have read these studies with real enrichment to my heart and mind, and I pray that they may be the means under God of thrusting many a sower into the harvest field who, 'bearing precious seed, shall doubtless come again with rejoicing, bringing his sheaves with him' (Ps. 126:6).

Gerald B. Griffiths

Charlotte Chapel
Edinburgh

Preface
to the second edition

It is nearly 50 years since I wrote the first edition of *God's Harvest*. Much has changed since then. In Wales less than 8.6% of the population attends a place of worship and the ravages of the defection from the Christian faith appear more severe than in any other part of Britain. Therefore, I have no hesitation in saying that the need for revival in Wales is greater now than it was half a century ago. That is one good reason for publishing a new edition of this book.

A second reason is that during the 35 years I have spent in the United States I have read a lot of American literature on revival and its effects. It was one of our previous Presidents, Calvin Coolidge, who said that 'America was born in a revival of religion. Back of that revival were John Wesley, George Whitefield and Francis Asbury'. However, in recent years, revival has had a bad press in America—as it has in Britain. As a result, many people associate it with men such as Elmer Gantry. Others link it with extreme forms of mass emotionalism.

The purpose of this book is to correct such misconceptions by outlining what the Scriptures teach about revival. However, in doing so it is good to remind ourselves that if our study of revival is to be profitable, it has to involve more than historical or intellectual interest. We are not meant to pursue such a study with the luxury of detachment, for it confronts us with a divine challenge: 'Why have we not known this?' It is meant to search us and it can be an uncomfortable experience—but its purpose is to create in us a clearer understanding of God's greatness and a hunger and thirst after righteousness which drives us to the place of penitence and of prayer.

Faced with our great spiritual needs and those of our nations, may a right understanding of God-given revival and its effects keep us from despondency and despair and bring us before the throne of God with the urgent and unceasing cry 'Will you not revive us again, that your people may rejoice in you?' (Ps. 85:6 NIV).

I. D. E. Thomas
January 1997

1
The plowman overtaketh

Wales is the proud possessor of many titles. She has been called *'the land of song'*, for poetry and singing have characterized the life of her people for many centuries. She has long been famous for alliterative lines and metrical verses, her choirs and her choruses, her congregational singing and her inspired hymnology. In the succinct language of the National Eisteddfod motto, *'Môr o gân yw Cymru i gyd'*: the land of Wales is a sea of song.

She has also been called *'the land of the white gloves'*. This arose from the custom when a judge visited a court of law, and there were no criminal cases for trial, to present him with a pair of white gloves. Therefore, it is an eloquent testimony to the moral and social effects of revivals of the Christian faith on the nation in years gone by, that she should have been given this title. One prominent Welshman suggested that a pair of white gloves should be substituted for the red dragon on the national flag of Wales. From the stand-point of apocalyptic literature, such a suggestion would find much commendation! Sadly, more recent history has shown such a suggestion to have been inappropriate—even for Wales!

What has brought the nation most honour, however, is that she has been called *'the land of revivals'*. It is from these that her true greatness stems. Were it not for the revivals with which God blessed her, most of her songs would be uninspired and most of her hymns unwritten. Just as he inspired the Psalmist in Israel, it is God who 'hath put a new song' (Ps. 40:3) in *our* mouth too. It was during periods of revival that the land resounded with the praises of God and men and women learned to respect and care for one another. It was then that the chapels were full, and the courts of law were empty.

It is probably true to say that no other country in the world has a greater claim to be called the land of revivals than has Wales. From the fourteenth century onwards, we read of men being raised up by God in generation after generation to lead their people from sin, superstition and ignorance, to the knowledge and experience of salvation in Jesus Christ. The eighteenth century saw the great Methodist Revival, which left an indelible mark upon the life and history of the nation. It is interesting to note here that the leaders of that revival—as of many others—were young men in their early twenties when the revival started: in 1738, Daniel Rowlands and Howell Harris were 24, whilst William Williams of Pantycelyn was only 21! From 1785 to 1904 Wales experienced no less than 16 revivals, and although some of these were localized and limited in extent, their influence on individuals and on districts was profound. In 1904–05 the nation experienced her last great revival, when Evan Roberts and others were called of God to be the human agencies for spreading the revival flame throughout the length and breadth of the land.

Seeing then that we have such a rich heritage of revivals, and that the most urgent need of our age is for God again to 'rend the heavens and come down' (Isa. 64:1,2), it is pertinent that

14

we should study afresh the teaching of the Word of God concerning revival. What exactly is meant by a revival? How is the word defined, and what are the principles involved?

Revival

Dictionaries easily define the verb *to revive*, but have difficulty in defining the noun *revival* in its religious context. One dictionary defines *revival* as the *return of life*. Others define it as *an act of reviving after decline*, or *recovery from apparent death*. These two definitions are more acceptable than the first, because they teach that true Christians never decline into a state of actual spiritual death, but only into *apparent death*. Revival therefore means recovery from a state of apparent death into a state of spiritual virility and fullness of life. However, all three definitions agree on one point—revival is confined to those who have already received spiritual life from God. It is only people who have been born again by the Spirit of God (John 3:5f.) who can be *re*vived. Therefore, revival is a term applicable only to the Church as the body of Christ (1 Cor. 12:12f.; Eph. 4:15,16).

This is one of the main differences between revival and evangelism. Revival primarily deals with the need of the Church; evangelism with the need of the world. Evangelism aims to reach people who have no spiritual life at all, but who are 'dead in trespasses and sins' (Eph. 2:1). Did not John Ruskin once define preaching as 'thirty minutes to raise the dead'? So evangelism can be defined as *rescuing people from death*, and revival as *recovering people from apparent death*. Having made this distinction, one should also bear in mind that every true revival results in great evangelism. Christians who have been revived are anxious to bear witness to the saving grace of God to the world—and this leads to a great ingathering of souls. The Holy Spirit uses a revival not only to revive the saints but also to save sinners, and through it all brings glory to the Lord Jesus Christ (John 16:14).

In the last analysis however, any attempt to define revival leaves one with the feeling that there are certain words in our vocabulary which are better described than defined. And 'revival' is in that category. This may be one reason why the Bible gives us no precise definition of revival, but prefers the picturesque colours of description to the stolid technicalities of definition.

One example of such a description is given by the prophet Amos, 'Behold, the days come, saith the Lord, that the plowman shall overtake the reaper, and the treader of grapes him that soweth seed' (9:13 AV). This description emphasizes a truth which we tend to forget, namely, that the distinguishing mark of every true revival is that it is entirely beyond the control of human beings. It is important to emphasize this fact before elaborating upon the believer's responsibility in revival.

In the harvest, portrayed so vividly by Amos, the seed which was sown has resulted in a harvest of supernatural dimensions. The sower sows the seed, and then the reaper reaps the harvest, and continues to reap—even after the plowman has arrived in the field to prepare for the following year's harvest! An ordinary sowing results in an extraordinary reaping! It is immediately obvious that such a transformation is the work of God and is beyond all human control. So it is with a revival. Just as such a harvest cannot be accounted for in terms of human ingenuity, so no true revival can ever be initiated by human planning or controlled by human planning and organizing.

It seems to be a characteristic of all revivals that they gloriously disorganize all preconceived plans and blueprints. This is to be expected, since the plan is always in the hands of God, and not of people. This is how Dr Campbell Morgan describes the last Welsh Revival: 'In connection with the awakening, there is no preaching, no order, no hymn-books, no choirs, no organ, no collections, and finally no advertising . . . yet the Welsh Revival is the revival of preaching to Wales. Everybody is preaching. No order, yet it moves from day to day, week to week, county to county, with matchless precision, with the order of an attacking force. No choir, but it was all choir . . .' Further study of Amos 9:13 shows that there are four key factors in every true revival, which are beyond human control.

1. *Its duration*

It is impossible for any one to plan a time-table, or set a time-limit for a revival. No man can predict the day of its commencement, nor the hour of its termination. Just as the reaper remains in the field, far beyond the time of normal harvest, so a revival may continue unabated for many weeks or many months.

With other programmes, we normally announce the day on which they are to start, and the day on which they are to finish. Even our evangelistic campaigns have to conform to human time-tables. But not so a revival; it refuses to comply with man-made schemes, and remains immune to the dictates of committees. The commencement and duration of a revival are beyond human control.

Everyone has seen brightly-coloured posters announcing 'revival meetings' about to be held in a locality. We are told the exact date they are to start, and the exact date they are to finish. But this is presumption: sinners daring to claim the work of the Almighty! Only those profoundly ignorant of the working of the Holy Spirit speak of revival in this way.

2. *Its location*

No one can tell, with any certainty, where a revival will break out. It has often started in the most unexpected place, and amongst the most unlikely people. The Lord speaks of the Holy Spirit as Sovereign: 'The wind bloweth where it listeth and thou hearest the sound thereof, but canst not tell whence it cometh, and whither it goeth' (John 3:8). A harvest of supernatural dimensions may be reaped in the most unpromising field. Whilst it is true to say that God normally works through his people—those who are sensitive to his will and obedient to his commands—but there are times when he seems to work in spite of his people, rather than through them. That is why it is not possible from a human standpoint to decide the location of any future revival and whom God will use as his channels.

When revival came to one Welsh city in 1904, it started in most unexpected quarters. This city has a University College, a number of theological colleges, a Cathedral church, large Protestant chapels, suggesting that if revival should come to the city, it would start in one of these noted centres. But God

18

thought differently. When the revival came, it by-passed these centres of learning and religion, and started in a small mission church, amongst some of the most poor and insignificant people of the city. Later, it spread further afield, but who could have foretold where it would start?

3. *Its momentum*

Amos tells us that the plowman *overtakes* the reaper, and the treader of grapes *overtakes* him that sows seed (9:13). In revival things happen with such a momentum, that many of our ordinary Christian organizations and denominational set-ups are incapable of coping with them. The form and rapidity of events is such that much of our church machinery is thrown out of gear.

One church in South Wales used to accept an average of 15 people into membership in a normal year prior to the revival, but in 1905 it accepted a total of 318. It is estimated that 20,000 people joined the churches during the first five weeks of the revival, and that during the first two months of Evan Roberts's tour of Glamorgan over 80,000 responded to the gospel. Similar happenings have accompanied other revivals of religion. When Charles G. Finney visited Rochester, NY, it is reported that 100,000 people were added to the churches. It is interesting to remember that when Finney was raised up, there were only 200,000 church members in the whole of the United States, but a few years later, when his work was finished, the numbers had risen to over three million. How, except through a God-given revival, can such a thing happen?

The harvest we normally experience is very slow to ripen and scanty in fruit, but when God sends a revival the harvest reaches unmanageable proportions. The divine initiative quickens the whole growth. One Welsh minister, asked to define a miracle, stated that it was 'the acceleration of a natural process'. The first of Christ's miracles was to turn water into wine at Cana in Galilee, but, he said, water is turned into wine every year in the vineyards of France. The water comes down from the clouds, is absorbed by the roots of the vine, is sent up into the branches in sap that fills the clusters, which are eventually converted into wine. But what takes normally many months to accomplish, Christ accomplished in a moment! The natural process was accelerated!

This same miraculous element is found in revivals. One man observed that 'God accomplished more in a single day of revival than he had accomplished during the whole of my ministry.' Such momentum bears witness that this is the work of God

4. *Its Infection*

This harvest was not confined to the field: it spread to the vineyard as well: 'the treader of grapes [overtakes] him that soweth seed' (Amos. 9:13).

In every revival, Christianity becomes highly infectious; and the influence spreads. We have already noted one of the differences between a revival and an evangelistic campaign, namely the difference in who is in control, but here is another difference—difference in the method of operation. In a revival, the human element is neither as apparent nor as important as it is in evangelism. In modern evangelistic campaigns, there is a well-known evangelist, of national or even international repute, and he may be supported by a team of specialists, including soloists, organists, choirs, personal workers, ushers, etc. There is usually vast and expensive publicity, a carefully drawn-out plan, a number of preliminary meetings, and all sorts of means are used in order to attract the people.

In revival, however, the human element is not nearly so apparent; there may be no publicity, no pre-conceived plan, no team of specialists, and even the leader himself may be an ordinary, insignificant person. Evan Roberts was a young ministerial student at a preparatory school, and even his most ardent admirers would admit that he was a man of limited gifts. Prior to 1904 he was unknown, and after 1905 he went into seclusion. Evan Roberts's strength was not in himself. The powerful effects of a revival are not dependent on human personalities. That is why Evan Roberts came away from many meetings without having uttered a word, and yet the people were converted. There were times when monoglot Englishmen were converted in meetings carried on entirely in the Welsh language. At other times, Roberts would leave the district, but the revival would go on, and often greater work was accomplished after his departure than when he was present. How can these things be explained except by the fact that the control of a revival is in the hands of God alone, and therefore it is able to proceed on its course without being dependent on human agencies.

Another feature of revival, which corroborates this truth, is the way in which people respond to a 'gospel appeal'. In a campaign, an evangelist appeals to the people, even to the point of coaxing them, to accept the Lord Jesus Christ as their personal Saviour. If half-a-dozen respond, he may feel quite pleased. It is not in every meeting that a man may gather such fruit by his labours. In a revival however, the whole situation is different. It is not a case of half-a-dozen, but of crowds of people experiencing deep conviction of sin so that concern for their souls becomes a matter of life and death. The whole atmosphere becomes charged with terrifying conviction, heart-rending confessions and mounting fervour, as the very flood-gates of heaven are thrown open wide. At such times the Christian faith becomes highly infectious.

The world has always found difficulty in understanding this infectious element in revival. In the eighteenth century it was called *enthusiasm*, and those who responded to it were dubbed *enthusiasts*. The word was used derisively. In Acts 2:13, the apostles were accused of being 'full of new wine'—of *drunkenness*. In Acts 26:24, the accusation was that of *madness*: 'Paul, thou art beside thyself; much learning doth make thee mad.' In the state of drunkenness or madness, people are not in full control of themselves, they are under some other influence, or in the grip of some other power. The world was right in asserting that the apostles were under the control of some other power: their error lay in identifying that power as a disordered mind and not the Spirit of God.

What happened on the day of Pentecost has happened again and again in times of revival. God, through the Holy Spirit has taken control, and so used men and women that the results have been extraordinary. Many have become acutely aware of their spiritual needs. Many have sought God, not in crowded meetings, but in the solitude of fields or in the seclusion of their own rooms. They have cried out, as did the Jews at Pentecost, 'What shall we do?' (Acts 2:37), and have been brought to seek forgiveness from their Saviour and been born again by the Spirit of God. At the same time, the lives of many of God's people have been transformed through a deepened relationship with their God. Prayer has reached into an altogether new dimension of communion with God, and reading the Bible has become as if its very words were aflame with light. This is the spiritual fulfilment of the harvest prophesied by Amos, when 'the plowman shall overtake the reaper, and the treader of grapes him that soweth seed.'

2
At the gate

We have already seen that the distinguishing mark of every true revival is that it is beyond human control —that God has reserved it for himself. Having said this, are we then to assume that God's people have no part at all to perform in relation to a revival? Is it simply left to them to sit down, and to wait with folded arms for God to do the work? God forbid. God's people have a very definite task to perform—and even if no revival is forthcoming there is not a single day in which they are free from this responsibility. Although they cannot *plan* a revival—they are bidden to *prepare* for it; although they cannot *organize* it—they are to *agonize* for it. This is their great task, always to be preparing themselves for a supernatural harvest such as that portrayed so vividly by the prophet Amos: the day when 'the plowman shall overtake the reaper, and the treader of grapes him that soweth seed' (9:13).

Preparing for revival

In what way then are we to prepare for revival? What exactly are we to do as we wait for this supernatural harvest? Are we not to continue with the normal tasks of an ordinary harvest, but always praying that in God's time he will bless us with an *extraordinary* one? This, surely, is the task to which we have been called: to plough the fields, to scatter the seed and to reap the crops. We are to be the Lord's faithful servants—whether the harvest is meagre or abundant!

As we consider our task as harvesters there are certain preparations which we should make before we actually enter on the field. The harvesters must prepare *themselves* before participating in the harvesting of others. When they appear at the gate, ready to enter the field, they must be adequately equipped for the task before them.

If we look again at the way that God established his Church, we note that originally Pentecost (Acts 2:1) was the Feast of Harvest and the Day of First-fruits. There could hardly be a more appropriate type of the first ingathering of a glorious harvest of souls! It should be profitable, therefore, if we examine how the apostles prepared themselves for entering this harvest field. What were the means which they used? For in spite of the multitude of changes which have occurred since then, the means whereby God's people are to prepare themselves for his service remain the same. Modern devices and sophisticated methods are no substitutes for the means of grace which God has provided. How then did they prepare themselves—and how are we to prepare ourselves?

Among other things we read in the Book of Acts that:

1. They assembled in the right attitude of fellowship.

'These all continued with one accord . . . And when the day of Pentecost was fully come, they were all with one accord in one place' (1:14; 2:1).

26

Two remarkable facts are recorded in these verses! They were *all* present, and present with *one* accord: the fellowship was complete, and there was complete fellowship! How important it is, if we sincerely desire a true revival, that there should be complete harmony within our churches. God alone knows the blessings that have been lost to the church because of unresolved differences and strained relationships amongst her members.

We are living in days when great stress is put on ecumenicity. It has become a popular cry that there should be unity between the churches, and that they should all come together for the formation of one mammoth church—'One world, one church'. But, however great the need for genuine unity *between* the churches, there is one greater and more vital need, namely, that there should be real unity *within* the churches. That should be the first task of every church today in preparing for revival. Every spirit of animosity, contention and bitterness should be shed, and peace, unity and mutual love should be assiduously cultivated (Phil. 2:1f.). This is what the disciples did: they came together 'with one accord' (Acts 1:14; 2:1). It had not always been so among them. They had been guilty of disputes and jealousy—and that even at the Lord's table (Luke 22:24). Even there, the recurring question as to which of them should be greatest raised its ugly head. We find, that even after the resurrection Peter is still restive about John's position (John 21:21). Happily, however, on the day of Pentecost they are together with 'one accord'. Even the way in which the apostles are listed is significant: in the Gospels it used to be 'Peter and James and John'. Now it is 'Peter and John and James . . .' (Acts 1:13). This new depth of unity which the apostles entered into meant that Peter and John could be coupled together. All personal animosities disappeared—pride of place gave way to penitence of heart, and self-seeking was replaced by a mutual devotion of their risen, glorified Saviour!

Are we in true fellowship with our fellow-Christians? Are we right with each one, or do we harbour feelings of envy and bitterness towards some? Are we guilty of an unforgiving spirit, or an undying grudge? Have we a ready tongue for slander or itching ears for gossip? Is there a fountain of jealousy allowed within our hearts, spreading poison in all directions? Except we be right with fellow-Christians how can we expect the blessing of God on our lives and on our efforts? (1 John 4:20).

Some people find it easier to be supposedly right with God than to be right with their fellow-believers. It is so much easier to go and confess a wrong secretly to God than to go and do so openly to another. Such was Jacob's experience. At Bethel he received God's promise, 'I am with thee, and will keep thee . . .' (Gen. 8:13f.). Then Jacob vowed a vow to God, and departing from Bethel he continued on his journey to Mesopotamia. But not for twenty years did he return to his brother Esau and ask his forgiveness for the deceit and treachery which he and his mother had perpetrated. On his return journey, however, he has the experience of Penuel (Gen. 32), and from Penuel he goes out to meet his brother (Gen. 33). But what a long time it took Jacob to go from Bethel to Penuel! From being 'in the house of God' to seeing 'the face of God'!

What a difference it would make to our church meetings if the spiritual climate was what it should be, if all the members were of 'one mind' and 'one accord'! What a difference it would make to the preaching of the Word, if the prevailing atmosphere was one of unity and prayer! It was in such an atmosphere that Peter preached on Pentecost. The Rev. W. Middleton used to assert that the chief reason for Peter's success—as contrasted with Paul's apparent failure on Mars Hill—was that Peter was surrounded by one hundred and twenty believers who were all filled with the Holy Ghost. Paul, on the other hand was alone, and had no band of Christian intercessors surrounding him with their prayers, with one heart and mind calling upon God, in his mercy and power, to give effect to his words. How important it is that all church members should realize their responsibility for creating a healthy spiritual climate for the preaching of the Word. Those who preach the gospel need such a climate today just as much as they did in the early church! If ministers were surrounded by praying Christians, many who are now deeply discouraged by difficulties and fruitlessness would surely know a heaven-sent quickening of their spiritual life and ministry.

If the church is not prospering in these days, let not all the blame be put on ministers. The unhealthiness of the spiritual climate in which they labour must be a contributing factor. Even the Son of God could not do many mighty works in his own country 'because of unbelief' (Matt. 13:58). One Welsh commentator puts it like this: 'The coldness of the people of Capernaum palsied the arm of the blessed Saviour, and froze his loving words on his lips. A cold church, an unbelieving church, robs itself of the choicest blessings of heaven . . . roses will not grow in Greenland, trees will not blossom at the North Pole.' There is nothing that so damps a minister's spirit as does a cold and prayer-less congregation, unsympathetic to the gospel's demands and unresponsive to its promises. O that the wind of heaven would blow upon the Lord's garden in these days. 'Awake, O north wind, and come, thou south; blow upon my garden, that the spices thereof may flow out.' (Song 4:16).

2. They prayed with the right persistency

'These all continued with one accord in prayer and supplication' Acts 1:14); or as the New American Standard Version states: *'These all with one mind were continually devoting themselves to prayer.'*

The persistent prayer which preceded Pentecost is the God-given way of preparing for his blessing. Therefore, it is not surprising to find that preceding every great revival is great praying. As one peruses the history of revivals, one continually meets with this fact of prayer. It is important then to ask: what is the nature of this prayer for revival? What is its essence? The prayer life of many present-day Christians could be described as the repetition of certain words, at a certain time, in a certain posture. But these three elements do not constitute the essence of prayer.

There are times, of course, when it is necessary to clothe our thoughts in *words*, and to lead others in public prayer. However, devout Roman Catholics repeat the Paternoster fifteen times in the rosary, and the Ave Maria one hundred and fifty times! But our Lord reminds us that we shall not be heard for our 'vain repetitions' nor for our 'much speaking'. It is important to bear in mind that the essence of prayer does not consist in multiplicity of words and that prayer can be offered without audible words.

Neither does the efficacy of prayer depend upon its being

offered at a particular *time*. It does not matter whether our prayer-time be early morning, mid-day, or evening: neither the timing nor the time spent in prayer are the all-important factors. Of course one is well aware that the tendency today is to spend very little time in prayer. The prayer-life of many Christians seems to be condensed into an occasional church prayer-meeting, or into the reciting of a few phrases at bed-time. How meagre this is compared with the time spent in prayer by some of God's choicest saints! It is said of John Welch (son-in-law to John Knox) that 'he counted that day ill-spent in which seven or eight hours were not used alone with God, in prayer and the study of his Word' and it has been said of both Richard Baxter and John Fletcher that they 'stained their study walls with praying breath'. They were following the Lord's command 'that men ought always to pray, and not to faint' (Luke 18:1). It is essential to spend time with God in prayer if we are to be effective in the spiritual battle. Having said that, we still have to remember that the time-element as such does not constitute the essence of prayer.

Neither is our *posture* at prayer all-important. It is a good practice to go on our knees when we pray to God. Such posture can aid humility and submissiveness, but it is far from being the all-important element in prayer. It is possible to use the correct language, to spend much time, and to be in an appropriate position whilst praying, and in spite of all these things, not to have prayed at all.

What then is the fundamental characteristic of the prayer of the early apostles and the saints of God throughout the ages? We believe that the answer is to be found in the adjectives used to describe the apostles' praying in Acts chapter 1. Their

31

praying was 'continued', 'steadfast', 'earnest'. Their whole personality was taken up with praying; their whole attention was focussed on coming before God. Praying had priority over everything else. Their praying was not the mumbling of some formal petitions nor the reciting of pious phrases learned in childhood, but an expression of the deepest yearning in their life. What their hearts longed for, their words expressed before the throne of God.

One of the reasons that so many of our prayers go unanswered is that they do not faithfully express the real desires of our hearts. We may ask for most noble and worthy things, but unless those things are the actual desires of our hearts, then it is not prayer we are offering. When the apostles prayed, we read that they prefaced their prayer with the recognition of the fact that God not only hears our words but knows our hearts (Acts 1:24). And so they prayed without pretending, without trying to hide anything, but expressing that which they knew God could see to be their deepest longings.

It is essential then that prayer for spiritual revival—as indeed all prayer—should express that which is in our hearts. It is only then that it becomes real to us and acceptable to God. To change the metaphor, prayer should be the external expression of the fire within our bones.

> *Prayer is the soul's sincere desire,*
> *Uttered or unexpressed,*
> *The motion of a hidden fire*
> *That trembles in the breast.*
>
> (James Montgomery)

It is only this kind of praying which can be offered 'continually' (Acts 1:14 NASV); at all times (Eph. 6:18 NASV). It does not end when our words end, but lives on as the desire of our hearts, the thought of our minds, and the object of our will—and it goes on being heard by God!

It is in this respect that we are to imitate the great men of prayer. It is not intended that we should imitate their phraseology, nor the exact length of time they spent on their knees, but we should imitate them in making the object of our praying the dominant yearning of our life. These great saints longed to see their Lord honoured, and for the fulfilment of that one thing they were willing to sacrifice every other thing. When prayer is rooted in such conviction and such love, it becomes the most irresistible force in the world.

It is in such a light that we should understand the prayer of John Knox, when he cried out, 'God, give me Scotland, or I die!' Or the prayer of the apostle Paul, when he said, 'my heart's desire and my supplication to God is for them, that they may be saved' (Rom. 10:1). When we pray for revival, does our praying spring from love for God and a deep desire to see his Son glorified—and is that the dominant desire in our life? It is then that our praying will be like the praying at Pentecost: 'continued', 'steadfast' and 'earnest'. It is such prayer that is prevailing prayer.

3. They reasoned from the right basis

'. . . This Scripture must needs have been fulfilled' (Acts 1:16).

During the interval between the ascension of the Lord Jesus Christ and the coming of the Holy Spirit at Pentecost, the disciples were concerned with the problem of Judas. How were they to interpret his betrayal of the Lord and his subsequent death?

A few weeks earlier when the risen Christ joined the company of the two disciples who had left Jerusalem and were walking to Emmaus, we are told that 'He expounded unto them in all the Scriptures the things concerning himself' (Luke 24:27). This is the example which Peter now follows as they discuss the death of Judas. He quotes from the Psalms an explanation of what had taken place (Ps. 69:25 and 109:8). David was referring to one of his own enemies in these psalms, and was probably unaware of the 'full richness of their Messianic content'. Peter, however, deliberately quotes these verses with reference to Judas. Again and again in the Acts we find the apostles having recourse to the Scriptures, and finding in them light for their problems and authority for their assertions. This was the basis on which Paul always reasoned: he 'reasoned with them out of the Scriptures' (Acts 17:2). To the apostles the Scriptures were God's Word: when the Scriptures spoke, God spoke. Every line was stamped with the autograph of the only true God. The apostles showed none of the hesitancy and diffidence of so many present-day theologians and preachers. Their preaching was always positive and full of assurance, in the great tradition of the Hebrew prophets. But, whereas the prophets would say, 'Thus saith the Lord', the apostles would say 'Thus saith the Scriptures'.

In every revival, when it has pleased God to quicken his Church, one of the instruments of that revival has been the Holy Scriptures. We find this in the Old Testament. When Hilkiah the High Priest found the long lost Book of the Law, its discovery led to a deep and far-reaching revival of religion (2 Chr. 34). It was the same in the days of Ezra. Before coming to Jerusalem to inaugurate the work of reformation, 'he had prepared his heart to seek the law of the Lord, and to do it, and to teach in Israel statutes and judgments' (Ezra 7:10).

More than once during its history the Christian Church has been near to death, but every time she has found in the Bible the way back to the God of revival and renewal. When at times she has been guilty of substituting social ethics for her Christian message, it is God's Word that has called her back. And, today when she is being made impotent by the inroads of modernism and secular humanism, it is the Bible that still shows her the remedy. Indeed it is difficult to imagine the Church existing at all without the Bible. In our day she may have departed a long way from the New Testament pattern of a Church, but what would be her condition if she had no pattern at all? She would long ago have degenerated into an 'irrecognizable caricature'.

Since the Holy Scriptures are so vital to the life of the Church, it is not surprising to find that the channels which God uses in revival are those men and women who know God's Word and whose message and reasoning are derived faithfully from it. Those who have 'hid the Word' in their own hearts are the ones to expound it to others. No other spiritual exercise should give us greater joy than to know the Word of God. 'How sweet are thy words unto my taste! Yea, sweeter than honey to my mouth' (Ps. 119:103). No other exercise pays a richer spiritual dividend than the prayerful study of the Bible. It is in the place of prayerful study of God's Word that the foundation for spiritual victories is laid. Long before the armies clash in open battle, there have been secret consultations in the general's office! Before winning others into the kingdom of God, there has to be prayer and study in the secret chamber. It is to those who so prepare themselves that God gives victories.

It should also be borne in mind that it is to such people that the world will turn in their hour of need. They may at present be treated with indifference or even with contempt, and they will continue to be so treated until men and women recognize their desperate need. But once that spiritual need is realized, then the people of the Word will come into their own, and it is to them that the needy will go for enlightenment and counsel. For example, there used to work in one of the coalmines of South Wales a miner who had the reputation of being a student of the Word. For months he went unheeded and unwanted. But when the revival broke out towards the end of 1904, he arrived at the mine one day to find one of the senior managers of the coalmine waiting for him. The manager said, 'Jim, I've been waiting here two hours for you.' 'Have you, sir?' answered Jim. 'What do you want with me?' 'I want to be saved', was the answer. And there and then, the manager was instructed by the Bible-believing miner, and passed into the kingdom of God. In their hour of spiritual need it is to men and women with an established reputation as people of God that the world will turn.

4. They relied on the right power

'But ye shall receive power, after that the Holy Ghost is come upon you' (Acts 1:8).

How easy it would have been for the disciples, inspired by

the fact of their Lord's resurrection, to have gone out immediately to proclaim the gospel. But what if they had done so?
They would not have seen a harvest of three thousand souls
in one day! Peter could have preached the same sermon, on the
same street, to the same crowd, but he would not have seen the
same results. Although they were united in fellowship, continued steadfast in prayer and reasoned from the Scriptures,
they still lacked one thing without which there could be no pen-
tecostal harvest. They lacked *power*. So, we find them waiting
in Jerusalem, until they received 'the promise of the Father' (Acts
1:4). They knew that without the Holy Spirit they could achieve
nothing, for their Lord had told them that it was only when he
came upon them that they could be witnesses to him (Acts 1:8).
'Even the Bible,' said Coleridge, 'without the Holy Spirit, is like
a sundial by moonlight.'

The most perfect organization, the most attractive pro-
gramme, the most able preachers, are all useless unless we
are endued with the 'power of the Holy Spirit'. General Booth
believed that one of the chief dangers which confronted the present century was 'religion without the Holy Ghost'. How fool-
ish we are to put our faith in all sorts of schemes and movements,
and to be slow of heart to accept that our only effective source
of power is the Spirit of God.

A startling transformation took place in the experience of the
apostles, once they received the power of the Holy Spirit. They
became new men and all fear of the Jews disappeared. A short
time before, Peter had been afraid to testify to a servant girl
(Luke 22:54f.), but now he stood up boldly before all the people
(Acts 2:14f.). The apostles' tongues were loosed and with God-
given courage and commitment they preached the gospel of

Jesus Christ. The Church was established and the work of teaching 'all nations' the gospel of Christ was begun.

As Christian men and women are we relying on the Holy Spirit's power today? Or is our power limited because we have 'grieved' or 'quenched' the Spirit (Eph. 4:30; 1 Thess. 5:18)? Without his power in our life, we shall not be able to sow or harvest and we shall not see the Lord adding to the Church those who are being saved (Acts 2:47). Every other power is insufficient for the task. Powers of oratory, thought, music and a whole range of other techniques have been tried and found lacking. As Dr Cynddylan Jones states, all these other powers

> had been tried before Jesus Christ came into the world, and had been found wanting. Demosthenes, the prince of orators, had lived and died, and the world was unredeemed. Plato, the prince of thinkers, had lived and died, and the world was unredeemed. Aristotle, the prince of logicians had lived and died, and the world was unredeemed. Homer, the prince of poets, had lived and died, and the world was unredeemed. If man is to be saved, a new power must come into the field.

On the day of Pentecost the Lord Jesus Christ 'having been exalted to the right hand of God, and having received from the Father the promise of the Holy Spirit' (Acts 2:33), sent the Spirit into the world for that very purpose. If, therefore, we long to see our Saviour glorified in and through his people, let us devote ourselves to obedient, believing prayer 'until the Spirit be poured upon us from on high, and the wilderness be a fruitful field' (Isa. 32:15).

A Prayer for Revival

'O God, send us the Holy Ghost! Give us both the breath of spiritual life and the fire of unconquerable zeal. O Thou art our God, answer us by fire, we pray Thee! Answer us both by wind and fire, and then we shall see Thee to be God indeed. The kingdom comes not, and the work is flagging. Oh, that Thou wouldst send the wind and the fire! Thou wilt do this when we are all of one accord, all believing, all expecting, all prepared by prayer.

'Lord, bring us to this waiting state! God, send us a season of glorious disorder. Oh, for a sweep of the wind that will set the seas in motion, and make our ironclad brethren, now lying so quietly at anchor, to roll from stem to stern!

'Oh, for the fire to fall again—fire which shall affect the most stolid! Oh, that such fire might first sit upon the disciples, and then fall on all around! O God, Thou art ready to work with us, today even as Thou didst then. Stay not, we beseech Thee, but work at once.

'Break down every barrier that hinders the incoming of Thy might! Give us now both hearts of flame and tongues of fire to preach Thy reconciling Word, for Jesus' sake! Amen!'

C. H. Spurgeon

3
On the field

Having seen how the Holy Spirit's descent at Pentecost transformed the disciples and equipped them to be witnesses to Jesus Christ we now turn our attention to what happens when they enter 'the field'. The Lord had made it clear that 'the field is the world' and the 'the good seed are the children of the kingdom' (Matt. 13:38), whom he sends into the world. At Pentecost that 'sending' and 'sowing' began. When Peter stood 'with the eleven' (Acts 2:14) and they began proclaiming Jesus of Nazareth as 'both Lord and Christ' (Acts 2:36) in Jerusalem, they did so in the confidence that they and their successors were commissioned and equipped to be witnesses to their Lord in Jerusalem, and in all Judea, and in Samaria, and unto the uttermost part of the earth (Acts 1:8). When a little while later the Jewish religious leaders 'commanded them not to speak at all nor teach in the name of Jesus', they had no hesitation in replying 'we cannot but speak the things we have seen and heard' (Acts 4:20) and 'we ought to obey God rather than men' (Acts 5:29).

Such boldness of speech and strength of conviction makes strange reading in our day. So many have lost that certainty of conviction and clarity of vision that was enjoyed by the early church. As a result, our trumpets give an certain sound. We belong to a timid and anaemic age when opinions have taken the place of convictions, and when men count it of greater importance and gain to accommodate their views to those of the world around them than to stand and suffer for the unchangeable gospel of Jesus Christ. Liberal theology has left the Christian Church permeated by doubt and scepticism, disbelief and infidelity. This is most apparent when we look at how the Church sees its role or 'mission' in society. Many of its members today have no idea why the Church exists, and no idea as to her primary task in the world. They work without any definite end in view, as if God had never revealed any purpose or given any commands to his people. Ignorance and doubt regarding the divine revelation and the mission of the Church to the world cripples its testimony and saps its courage. What a difference it makes to our approach to the work and to the methods we use when God's people are certain that the work in which we are engaged is the work which God has given his Church to do!

The mission of the Church

Let us therefore consider, first, what God *has not* given the Church to do and secondly, the task which God *has* given his Church to do in the field which is the world.

1. Wrong views

Some would have us believe that the primary task of the Church is to uphold and disseminate civilization, making its fruits available to all men everywhere. Her task is to *civilize* the barbarian and tame the savage. In other words, she is to be a handmaid to civilization, concerned with such things as culture, education, economics, and social amenities. And, on the local level, many churches seem to work to this end, giving far more prominence to cultural and recreational activities than to evangelism and prayer and Bible study.

However, God never intended his Church to be a mere handmaid to civilization, advanced or progressive though that civilization might be. According to Dr Arnold J. Toynbee, a leading authority on the study of history, the world has witnessed 21 civilizations, beginning with that of Egypt and ending with our modern Western civilization. Although they vary in many respects, there is one factor which is common to them all—they have all failed or are failing. The Church of the living God was never meant to identify itself with any of these, but to perform a task infinitely greater and far more permanent.

There are others who would have us believe that the primary function of the Church is that of *reforming* the world. She is to act as a 'change agent', concerned with improving moral standards, as well as the environment and human relationships.

It is surprising how many within the Church still believe that improvements in social circumstances and in the environment will inevitably lead to an improvement in people's characters. Their 'gospel' is that changes in character come from changes in the environment: that a better house and a better neighbourhood will change a sinner into a saint!

Desirable as such improvements undoubtedly are, time and again this theorizing has been proved as futile as the attempts which were made by the Gadarenes to deal with the man with an unclean spirit (Mark 5:3,4). They tried to change him from without, but always with the same result: no man could tame him (Matt. 5:4). The Evangelical Movement of the eighteenth century taught that true religion is 'the life of God in the soul of man, bearing fruit in every good work for human betterment.' Such is still the emphasis of biblical Christianity—understanding as it does that good works and human betterment are always the *fruit* and not the source of the life of God in the soul. The reformation of society is one of the by-products of a vibrant Christian faith, but it is not its primary task to bring it about.

There are others who maintain that the primary task of the Christian Church is that of *Christianizing* the world. Her aim should be the leavening of the whole world with the Christian ethic. They maintain that if the rulers of the nations based their policies on the principles expounded in the Sermon on the Mount, then we would see peace on earth, with swords being beaten into plowshares and spears into pruning-hooks. However, the Lord Jesus Christ did not deliver the Sermon on the Mount as a blueprint for the kingdoms of this world, but for the citizens of the Kingdom of God. It was delivered to the disciples and not to the multitude: 'And seeing the multitudes, he went up into a mountain and when he was set, his disciples came unto him: and he opened his mouth and taught *them*' (Matt. 5:1,2). It is only those who have already become citizens of the Kingdom who have the God-given inclination and power to live according to the principles of the Sermon on the Mount. It is only those who have the life of Christ who can obey the commands of Christ, and it is not therefore possible that the task of the Church should be to Christianize the world.

2. Biblical teaching

What then is the primary task of the Church? If it is not to civilize, nor to reform, nor to Christianize—for what purpose was she called into being and sent 'into the field'? For the answer, we turn to the words of the Lord Jesus Christ. At Caesarea Philippi he first declared it to be his purpose to 'build my church' (Matt. 16:18). Later, he reveals that this will be done as 'the gospel of the kingdom' is 'preached in all the world for a witness to all nations' (Matt. 24:14), and, finally, he reveals who will do it, when he commands his disciples: 'All power is given unto me in heaven and in earth. Go ye, therefore, and teach all nations . . . and, lo, I am with you alway, even unto the end of the world' (Matt. 28:18-21). As we have already seen, when the disciples receive the Holy Spirit at Pentecost, then they immediately become 'witnesses' to Jesus Christ (Acts 1:8).

So then, the primary task of the Church is to *evangelize*. It is to call out from amongst the nations a supra-national people 'for his name' (Acts 16:14). The root meaning of the Greek word for 'church'—*ecclesia*—is 'called out of'. The people who form the Church of Jesus Christ are people called out from the different races and nations of the world in order to be a new creation—the Church of God. As Paul writes to the Galatian church: 'There is neither Jew nor Greek, there

45

is neither bond nor free, there is neither male nor female: for ye are all one in Christ Jesus' (Gal. 3:28). The Church is a fellowship of people who have become one in nature through receiving the life of God through regeneration. Having been called out to be God's people, the Church is now to call out others, through the direction and enabling of the Holy Spirit. The true Church has recognized this to be its primary task for nearly two thousand years: living for God, proclaiming the Good News; preaching the Word. As a result, a man here and a woman there, a young boy here and a young girl there, have accepted Christ as their Saviour, and by doing so have entered his Church. All over the world this plan of God is progressing in Europe and Asia, Africa and America, God is calling out his people from amongst the different races and building a Church which is to be 'unto the praise of the glory of his grace' (Eph. 1:6).

It is therefore tragic that many churches and denominations pay little or no attention to this most important, God-appointed task. Not only so, but a number of churches have abandoned evangelism, denying the validity of the task in their zeal for inter-faith ecumenism! Other churches recognize the validity of the task, but relegate it to a committee or department of the church which organizes evangelistic events from time to time.

What a far cry all this is from the conviction and practice of the early church! For them evangelism was the concern of the whole church the whole time, and not for some of the church some of the time. They were convinced that it was the church's primary work and not merely one activity amongst many. They were convinced that the purpose of the Holy Spirit in coming upon them was to equip them to bear witness to their Lord and to glorify him (Acts 1:8; John 16:14). Therefore, even when they were severely persecuted and driven from their homes in Jerusalem, these Christians 'that were scattered abroad went everywhere preaching the word' (Acts 8:4). They were the seeds of God—blown into the field, and bearing fruit wherever they landed!

Many churches today seem not to understand what the early church clearly did—that the church which fails to evangelize has surrendered the right to continue in existence. It is disobedient to its Master and lives on borrowed time. 'Remember therefore from whence thou art fallen, and repent, and do the first works, or else I . . . will remove thy candlestick out of his place, except thou repent' (Rev. 2:5).

Evangelism and Revival

Finally, having earlier drawn a distinction between evangelism—as a work in which God's people take the initiative—and revival—as a work in which God takes the initiative—it is important to emphasize that evangelism and revival are not in any way in opposition to one another, but that they complement each other. They are both ways which God has used over the centuries to build his Church. It is important to recognize this for at least two reasons.

First, in the periods when there is no revival, such as Wales has experienced since 1905, and many other lands for even longer, it is easy on the one hand to despise 'the day of small things' (Zech. 4:10) and to become discouraged when we read of how much God accomplished in a short time during days of revival. Many of the returned exiles looked back to the past glories of the first temple and drew an unfavourable comparison with the second (Hag. 2:3). Looking back to the *past* induced a disposition to despise the *present*. The same temptation is as real today. We may look back to past seasons of the outpouring of the Holy Spirit, especially in Wales, make a comparison with the present, and settle down to await revival in what amounts to a spirit of resigned fatalism. We may read of the mighty revivals of past centuries and wistfully say, 'If only we had such revival today, things would be different.'

On the other hand, if our understanding of the task of building the Church is based only on our experience of 'the days of small things', then we will have no sense of the need of revival and no vision of what God can, and does, do when he revives his Church.

Secondly, both the New Testament and the later history of the Church show that when God revives his Church, evangelism flows from it just as it did on Pentecost, as we saw earlier. The same sources also show us that the condition of effective evangelism is that the message and the messengers are one. That there is consistency between what is proclaimed and what is practiced. The church of Thessalonica is a fine example, for not only did it become a centre from which 'sounded out the word of the Lord (1 Thess. 1:8) but the faith and the love which characterized their lives and fellowship bore testimony to the transforming power of the gospel which they proclaimed (1 Thess. 1:8f.; 4:9f.).

Whether we enter 'into the field' in days of great or small

things, the conditions are exactly the same. We are to prepare ourselves, so that we are as 'corn of wheat' ready to fall into the ground and die, in order that God might make us fruitful (John 12:24), working in us and through us to build up his Church.

4
In the barn

In the preceding chapters we saw that the Scriptures depict a revival as an extraordinary harvest in which the sovereign initiative of God is the key element—the plowman shall *overtake* the reaper (Amos 9:13). We considered how God's people should prepare themselves for this work—*at the gate.* Finally we saw what the precise work of harvesting involves—*on the field*—and that the unchanging task of the church is to plough and sow and reap—the normal processes of securing a harvest which God also graciously uses to add to his Church.

Let us now consider the final aspect of the picture given by Amos (9:13), the purpose of God in this harvest—that is, what the end-product is intended to be. What is to be gathered into *the barn*?

It will be clear from preceding chapters that I do not believe that the Erastian and Romanist view of the Church is derived from the Scriptures—that the Church is virtually coextensive with the community—but that it is a fellowship of regenerate, men and women 'which he purchased with his own blood' (Acts 20:28), 'called out from' the world, and standing over and against it. These are the Church—the people of God. However, this picture is not in itself complete, for God not only calls out his people *from* the world but calls them to go *into* the world. They are to be separate from the world, and yet they are to penetrate its life at innumerable points as an influential minority acting as 'salt and light' in the communities where they live (Matt. 5:13,14). They are to influence its life and standards through their Christ-like characters and witness to the truth and power of the gospel of Jesus Christ (Acts 1:8). They are men and women who have been called to be citizens of the kingdom of God, so as to be sent back into the world as the 'ambassadors of Christ' (2 Cor. 5:20).

What kind of people are such men and women meant to be? They have already responded to the call of the gospel and received salvation in and through Jesus Christ. They have been called out from the world and have been brought into the Church. What now? What is to be the distinctive characteristic in the lives which they lead amongst their friends and acquaintances? The answer to this question is given in the Scriptures, which tell us that the purpose of God for his people is to make them holy: 'You shall be holy, for I am holy' (1 Pet. 1:16 NASV). How different this is from other religions. Mohammedanism gives the place of honour to those who fight and fall in conflict. Hinduism gives it to those who have best observed ritual worship. But the one true God who reveals his own holiness in the Scriptures and his Son calls men and women to be holy. Holiness is to be the *sine qua non* of God's people, for without holiness 'no man shall see the Lord' (Heb. 12:14). This then is to be the distinctive characteristic of God's people. This is to be what identifies them as God's people as they live in this world—they are to be 'holiness unto the Lord'.

Holiness

But what is holiness? Of what does it consist, and how is it recognized? Morley, in his essay on Voltaire, stated that holiness is the 'deepest of all the words that defy definition'. To the average person the word 'holiness' has a musty tang of otherworldliness and asceticism and conjures up a totalitarian denial of all pleasure, and the suppression of all joy. To many to be 'holy' means living a life of rigid self-denial carried to extreme lengths and, therefore, the very mention of the word gives rise to deep unease.

Even in theological circles the word holiness has not had a smooth passage and it has suffered much from both misunderstanding and mis-statement. It has been used to connote all sorts of varied and strange practices. It has also been used to indicate an unhealthy and introverted form of piety that is always contemplating one's own conviction. Dr Martyn Lloyd-Jones states that these people 'are so busily occupied in taking their own spiritual temperature and in feeling their spiritual pulses that they forget the heavenly Physician.' It must have been such people who were described as being 'so heavenly-minded as to be of no earthly use'!

At other times 'holiness' has been used to indicate the very opposite mode of conduct. That is the conduct of people who ignored the apostle's injunction—'let every man examine himself' (1 Cor. 11:28) and who indulged without restraint in all sorts of sins, and, what was even worse, justified themselves in so doing. They claimed to sin so 'that grace may abound' (Rom. 6:1). They convinced themselves that they were 'free of the law' (Rom. 7:3), and so they justified their sinning by the most specious rationalization. They did unholy things in the name of holiness!

What then does the Bible mean when it commands us to 'be holy'? Surely God has not left such an important word without clear definition. It certainly cannot mean that holiness is something forbidding and repellent, damping all our aspirations for life, for did not the Lord declare that the purpose of his coming into the world was that we 'might have life and have it more abundantly' (John 10:15)? What then is holiness?

The Bible teaches that there are three strands in the one cord of holiness, reminding us of the words of Ecclesiastes that 'a threefold cord is not quickly broken' (4:12). These strands are not meant to be pitted against one another, as is so often done, but are to be taken together in a complementary fashion, in order to show the richness and depth of the holiness which God intends should be the distinctive characteristic of his people.

1. *Imputed holiness*

All Bible scholars agree that the root meaning of holiness is 'set apart'. The Hebrew term is *qadosh*, and this, with its cognates, is used no less than 605 times in the Old Testament. Under the Mosaic economy not only were there *persons* designated as holy, but also *things*, *places*, and *seasons*. For example, we read of holy vessels, holy water, holy garments, and holy days (Deut. 28; Lev. 16). These were different from all others of their class in that they were set apart and exclusively used for divine service. Therefore, when the Old Testament refers

54

to a person as being 'holy' or 'sanctified', the primary meaning is that the person has been set apart by God and for God.

The same meaning is carried through to the New Testament and is to be found in the word *'saint'*. All believers are called saints (e.g., Eph. 1:1). This was the ordinary appellation of the saved, and used much more frequently than the name Christian: the word 'saint' is used sixty-two times, 'Christian', three times. Every one who received the Holy Spirit was called a saint. Even the members of the church at Corinth were referred to as saints (1 Cor. 1:2), although we read that at the very time that Paul was writing to them they were guilty of many grievous sins. Chapter 1 tells us that there were quarrels and divisions among them. Chapter 3 says that they were worldly. Chapter 5 names a dreadful sin that remained unjudged among them. Chapter 6 chastizes them for taking their disputes before pagan courts. Chapter 11 accuses them of excessive drinking—and that at the Lord's Supper! But in spite of all these things they are still called saints. How is it possible, one might ask, for people guilty of such 'unsaintly' conduct to be called saints? How can such people be holy? The answer is, that their holiness is an *imputed* holiness. The moment men and women put their trust in Jesus Christ, God in his infinite mercy imputes to them the righteousness and the holiness of Christ. As Paul tells us: 'Of him are ye in Christ Jesus, who of God is made unto us wisdom, and righteousness, and sanctification, and redemption' (1 Cor. 1:30). Regenerate men and women are called saints and are holy because the holiness of Christ is imputed to them.

This doctrine of imputation is explicitly stated three times in Scripture:

1. The sin of Adam is imputed to his posterity (Rom. 5:12-14).
2. The sin of man is imputed to Christ (2 Cor. 5:21).
3. The righteousness of God is imputed to those who believe (Rom. 3:22).

Therefore, when the Bible refers to the holiness of believers it means that the holiness of Christ is imputed to them. Christ bore in his own body on the cross their sins, which were imputed to him, and having satisfied the just requirements of a holy God by his priceless sacrifice on their behalf, his righteousness is now imputed to everyone who puts their trust in him The imputation of holiness derives from the believers' position in Christ, rather than from their condition: it refers to their status rather than their state. Just as in Christ we who are guilty are regarded as justified (Rom. 8:1), so also in Christ we who are defiled are regarded as sanctified. God has not only forgiven our sin, but declared us righteous and holy in Christ. He has covered naked sinners with the white robe of Christ's righteousness, imputing to them what they could not gain for themselves. Henceforth God sees them only as clothed in the spotless and immaculate garments of his Son. This truth is stated very succinctly in Zinzendorf's hymn:

> *Jesu, Thy blood and righteousness*
> *My beauty are, my glorious dress.*

This emphasis on imputed holiness, when rightly understood, is an inspiration and incentive to good works and holiness of life. When it is made an excuse for indulging in sinful practices, it is only another instance of how rebellious sinners are capable of perverting a sublime doctrine and using it in a way which is wholly opposed to God's intention.

2. *Imparted holiness*

It is the unequivocal testimony of Scripture that God not only *imputes* holiness to believers, but *imparts* it. He not only *regards* us as holy but *makes* us holy. We are not only declared to be holy in law but are made holy by nature. This God does by imparting to us the very nature and righteousness of Christ himself.

Put another way, holiness is both ethical and experimental. We are not only to be regarded as holy because Christ died for us, but are to be made holy because Christ dwells in us! This was Paul's prayer to God on behalf of the Thessalonians: 'And the very God of peace sanctify you wholly; and I pray God your whole spirit and soul and body be preserved blameless unto the coming of our Lord Jesus Christ (1 Thess. 5:23). This imparting of holiness is as much the gift of God as is his imputing of holiness. In Ryder Smith's phrase, it is *'from* the Father, *by* the Son *through* the Spirit, to the Christian.'

Perfection and absolute holiness is the only standard that prevails with God, and no one by their own merits and by their own efforts can ever achieve it. No cultivation of piety and no attainment of sanctity will he ever succeed in achieving perfect holiness. God, knowing this, has made full provision, and by virtue of the cross of Christ not only declares believers to be holy, but makes them holy. It is the gift of God. God sanctifies us by working in us 'both to will and to do of his good pleasure' (Phil. 2:13).

It is now evident that holiness contains an experimental or

57

spiritual, as well as an ethical content. This is to be seen very clearly in the Welsh word for holiness, which is *glân*. This word means not only 'holiness' in the spiritual sense, but also 'cleanness' both in the moral and physical sense. This association of cleanliness with holiness is not something peculiarly Welsh, for it is biblical. For example, Paul, writing to the Thessalonians, asserts: 'For God hath not called us unto uncleanness, but unto holiness' (1 Thess. 4:7). Holiness is here used as the opposite of uncleanness: it is only the clean that are holy. This is what the prophet emphasizes when he exhorts the people, 'Be ye clean, that bear the vessels of the Lord' (Isa. 52:11). Holy vessels were to be borne by holy people, that is, people separated unto the Lord and characterized by clean lives.

The same truth is also seen in the prophet's account of his experience in the temple, when he saw God seated upon his throne, high and lifted up, 'and his train filled the temple' (Isa. 6:1f.). He heard the seraphim cry: 'Holy, holy, holy, is the Lord of hosts: the whole earth is full of his glory.' He felt the posts of the door moving, and the house filled with smoke. Then a sense of uncleanness fell upon the prophet and he cries out: 'Woe is me! for I am undone; because I am a man of unclean lips . . .' What is to happen now? God is thrice holy, and the prophet before him is a sinful, unclean, man. What is to be done? A live coal is taken from off the altar, and touches his lips, and then his iniquity is taken away and his sin purged. God then asks: 'Whom shall I send, and who will go for us?' The prophet answers: 'Here am I; send me.' He is now clean and so he is accepted, and commissioned as God's holy messenger: 'Go and tell this people . . .' (Isa. 6:9).

So we see that it is God who imputes holiness, and that it

is God also who imparts holiness to the believer. Therefore, the question which arises is: does the believer also have a part to perform in being made holy? Has the believer anything to do besides receiving that which God gives? There can be only one answer to this question in the light of Scripture: the believer has a vital part to perform in becoming holy, and this brings us to the third strand in the cord of holiness.

3. *Progressive holiness*

The imputing and imparting of holiness by God may be seen as the source of the development of holiness in the life of the believer. This is sometimes referred to as spiritual growth, at other times as progress towards perfection. For although the saints are already perfect by virtue of their standing in Christ (Phil. 3:15), they are still striving towards such perfection of character throughout their earthly lives (Phil. 3:12). Paul also exhorts his Corinthian readers: 'Let us cleanse ourselves from all filthiness of the flesh and spirit, perfecting holiness in the fear of God' (2 Cor. 7:1). Note the term 'perfecting holiness' which clearly indicates that the holiness of the believer is incomplete and can and should be improved. It is something to be cultivated as a moral quality, something that demands action on the part of believer. We are to cleanse ourselves.

Some evangelicals have tended to neglect this aspect of holiness. Holiness as a gift of God without any merit or effort in the believer has been emphasized to the exclusion of holiness as Christ-likeness which we are to strive for in our daily lives. In the Epistles, however, this aspect of holiness is continually stressed. Believers are urged to 'walk worthy' of their high calling in Christ Jesus (Eph. 4:1), for like Paul we have to reach forward and 'press toward the mark' (Phil. 3:14). Peter can find no more fitting exhortation with which to close his Epistle than to urge his readers to 'grow in grace, and in the knowledge of our Lord and Saviour Jesus Christ' (2 Pet. 3:18).

To state that holiness is something which believers receive passively, without any effort on their part, is to read the New Testament through the filtering lenses of a pet theory! The very words employed by the apostles in their exhortations indicate that there is struggle and effort. We are to *yield* our members servants to righteousness unto holiness' (Rom. 6:19). We are to *put off*, concerning our former way of life, the old man. We are to be *renewed* in the spirit of our mind, and to *put on* the new man (Eph. 4:22-25). In other passages believers are urged to 'seek those things which are above'; to 'set' their affections on things above; to 'mortify' their members . . .' (Col. 3:1-5); to put on 'as the elect of God . . . bowels of mercies, kindness, humbleness of mind . . .' (Col. 3:12).

Sometimes the metaphor used is that of *warfare*. For example, Paul calls us to 'be strong in the Lord and in the power of his might' (Eph. 6:10); and to 'put on the whole armour of God' (Eph. 6:11). Sometimes it is that of *walking*: 'see then that ye walk circumspectly' (Eph. 5:15). Sometimes it is that of *running*: 'so run that ye may obtain' (1 Cor. 9:24); 'let us lay aside every weight, and the sin which doth so easily beset us, and let us run with patience' (Heb. 12:1). Sometimes it is that of *watching*: 'watch ye' (1 Cor. 16:13; Revelation 3:2). Sometimes it is that of *standing*: 'stand ye' (Eph. 6:14; Josh. 2:3). In all these instances, and in many more, it is believers who are urged to do these things, and therefore it is impossible to escape the conviction that the believer has a vital part to perform in being made holy.

There is clear evidence that godly men and women have so understood this truth down the ages. Many saints have striven and struggled, watched and prayed, laboured and loved, all in order to grow in Christ-likeness. Some of them, in spite of adverse circumstances, and unprecedented difficulties have, by the power of the Holy Spirit within them, shown extraordinary holiness, and it is marvellous in our eyes. There are others who have purposely denied themselves many of the legitimate things of life, in order that in knowing their Lord better they might be more like him. We think of Henry Martyn choosing India before his 'beloved Lydia', David Brainerd, parting with every shred of comfort and making his bed under any tree, John Wesley doing 'his herculean work on six hours sleep a night: he retired always at 10 p.m. and rose at 4 a.m.! Yet he was indulgent in comparison with his friend, John Fletcher of Madeley, who trained himself to sleep only when he could not keep awake, and yet he carried an alert mind to a wide range of duties, and prayed and meditated through two whole nights of every week'! Such men 'hungered and thirsted after righteousness' (Matt. 5:4), believing that their Saviour is glorified when his blood-bought people bear 'much fruit' (John 15:5,8).

We have been called out from the world in order to be a holy people to the Lord—in order to experience and demonstrate the transforming power of redemptive grace in the world. Our hearts' desire and perennial task is to grow in holiness—in fruitfulness of character and conduct— until we 'come in the unity of the faith, and of the knowledge of the Son of God unto a perfect man, unto the measure of the stature of the fullness of Christ' (Eph. 4:13). Such glorious perfection will only be fully ours when we arrive in God's own presence in the glory. But knowing that our Saviour has died for us so that we might be 'like him', each who has this hope will purify himself or herself 'even as he is pure' (1 John 3:2,3).

May our hearts beat faster and our commitment to Christ-likeness be deepened as we look forward to that day when our Lord will present us to himself 'not having spot or wrinkle or any such thing . . . holy and without blemish' (Eph. 5:27). Through both ordinary and extraordinary means, in that day all God's harvest will be safely gathered into his barn!

Revival Comes to Wales
**The story of the 1859
Revival in Wales
Eifion Evans**

A moving and thrilling account of the mighty
working of God the Holy Spirit in Wales at the time
of the 1859 Revival, a year in which an estimated
110,000 were converted. 132pp.

Pursued by God
**A selective translation with notes of the
Welsh religious classic Theomemphus by
Williams Williams of Pantycelyn
Eifion Evans**

This remarkable work displays profound insight into the
Scriptures and a deep discernment in the realm
of Christian experience in times of
spiritual revival. 191pp.

*Howell Harris and the
Dawn of Revival*
Richard Bennett

Introduction by **D. M. Lloyd-Jones**

A study of the early spiritual life of Howell Harris and
the beginnings of the Great Awakening of the
eighteenth century in Wales. 212pp.